Surprised by Christmas

Stories Through Advent and Christmas

Richard W. Reifsnyder

CSS Publishing Company, Inc.
Lima, Ohio

SURPRISED BY CHRISTMAS

FIRST EDITION
Copyright © 2015
by CSS Publishing Co., Inc.

Library of Congress Cataloging-in-Publication Data

Reifsnyder, Richard W. (Richard William)
  Surprised by Christmas : stories through advent and Christmas / Richard W. Reifsnyder. -- First edition.
      pages cm
  ISBN 978-0-7880-2827-4 -- ISBN 0-7880-2827-8 (alk. paper) -- ISBN 978-0-7880-2828-1 (e-book) -- ISBN 0-7880-2828-6 (e-book) 1. Christmas. 2. Advent. I. Title.

  BV45.R45 2015
  242'.33--dc23

                                        2014046486

For more information about CSS Publishing Company resources, visit our website at www.csspub.com, email us at csr@csspub.com, or call (800) 241-4056.

e-book
ISBN-13: 978-0-7880-2828-1
ISBN-10: 0-7880-2828-6

ISBN-13: 978-0-7880-2827-4
ISBN-10: 0-7880-2827-8   PRINTED IN USA

To Lynn

Table of Contents

Preface

During most of the time that I have served as pastor of First Presbyterian Church of Winchester, Virginia, I have written a story instead of preaching a traditional sermon at our Christmas Eve service of lessons and carols. The story of Jesus' birth is so familiar, the expectations of something magical happening on Christmas Eve so high, that it is difficult to know what to say. All our words seem conventional and routine, when the event of Christmas was so unconventional and so surprising. It seemed that a story might better convey the unexpected news of God's incarnation in Jesus and of the ongoing way that God continues to startle us with his presence.

I have long been an admirer of Garrison Keillor's "Lake Wobegone" stories. He has his fun with religious pretense and convention, but at their best, his stories affirm a conviction that God works in the most ordinary and mundane of circumstances, often through and in spite of our best efforts. Christmas hardly ever matches the celebration we create in our minds. The celebration of Christmas often includes dealing with complicated family dynamics, disappointed hopes, and unrealistic expectations. Christian families struggle with how to balance the secular trappings with the sacred essence.

I hope that these stories convey some of that same spirit of a living God working through ordinary life experiences. Through the years, people in the congregation have encouraged me to collect these Christmas stories and make them available to others. Storytelling does not come naturally to me, but I have enjoyed trying my hand at this form. Each story draws on experiences I have had as a pastor. Nearly all of them include a Christmas carol, for I have found it is the music of Christmas that often best conveys the most profound understanding of the incarnation. My hope is that in these stories' narrative of ordinary people trying to make sense of their lives, you might find a message of the surprising grace of God, breaking into our world, providing comfort, encouragement, and joy.

Although the stories were originally told on Christmas Eve, they are also suitable for other occasions during the Advent and Christmas seasons. I have used them as part of an education event for church musicians and as the program for a community civic club meeting. They could be used as a devotional before choir rehearsal or at a women's or men's meeting or other church gatherings. With some creative adaptation several of them could be put in dramatic format for use in worship. They could be read and used as discussion starters regarding aspects of how we celebrate Christmas. For example, "The Gift" might stimulate talk about the meaning of gift giving, or "The Invitation" could lend itself to consideration of the stress of family dynamics at Christmastime.

I want to thank the congregation of First Presbyterian for their love and support during more than twenty years of ministry. I am grateful to Nancy Johnson, who made a careful reading and offered many valuable suggestions. Special thanks are due to my wife Lynn, who not only listened to these messages and made important improvements to the text, but whose love and Christian witness has been the light of my life.

Rich Reifsnyder
Epiphany 2014

Homecoming

It was now their eighth Christmas without children and dealing with it was getting harder each year. The questions had seemed incessant when they moved back six months ago in order for Keith to take the position of principal of the middle school. He had never imagined returning to his home town of Olivet, but to achieve that job at age 34 was a dream come true. And Marcey quickly found a position in a bank in a neighboring town.

But the questions grated on him like chalk scratching on a blackboard. "When are you going to start your family?" The grim truth was that what seemed so easy to others didn't happen for them. People were well meaning but it seemed that his old friends were all settled in so comfortably. Their children were beginning preschool and taking ballet. Saturdays were spent on the soccer field and carting the kids to birthday parties. Everyone complained about how busy it all was, how expensive diapers were, and how the kids' fighting was more than they could bear, but it seemed to Marcey and Keith as though grumbling about parenting was one of the perverse satisfactions of family life. And every conversation reminded them that they had no children's schedules to keep.

Every few months it seemed as though another teacher was getting pregnant and having a baby shower. The custom now was to invite couples and although they smiled and oohed and aahed over all the gifts, they would often return home feeling very alone.

Of course, it was particularly tough this Christmas. Nine weeks into her first pregnancy — which they hadn't even told many people about — Marcey began hemorrhaging. No one had to tell her; she just knew that she would lose the baby. Another Christmas without children; another Christmas watching families light the Advent wreath; another Christmas watching the nephews and nieces rip open their presents; another Christmas hearing all that baby talk in church and feeling left out.

Marcey wasn't sure she was up to going to church on Christmas Eve, but Keith persuaded her it would be good for them. They hadn't done any decorating — and frankly didn't feel much like it. So they ate a late supper, wrapped a couple of presents, and started off to the 11 p.m. candlelight service.

Keith had attended Saint Andrew's since he was six years old, more willingly at some times than others. His parents had divorced when he was thirteen — a tough age at best — and his mother seemed to have gotten the church in the settlement. His father tried for a while, but then gravitated to the Methodist church. Keith went with him when he spent every other weekend at his house, but after his dad's remarriage somehow it seemed less important. By contrast his mother was in church nearly every time the door opened. She seemed to need it even more after her marriage disintegrated. She made sure Keith was a regular at Sunday school and youth group and, except for a bit of typical adolescent grumbling about how unfair it was to have to get up so early on Sunday morning, he really didn't mind it.

But Christmas Eve was another matter. Maybe it was just the comforting glow of the candlelight; maybe it was all the college students home for the holidays; maybe it was all the grandparents taking up whole pews with the church regulars, but it seemed all around him were gathered big, happy, contented families. The longing within was deep for what he still missed, and what he still wanted, perhaps what all people want — the perfect family, all sitting together, experiencing in their life together, "Peace on earth, goodwill toward all." He knew enough to realize that perfect families are a myth. Families are rarely that simple, however intact they may appear on the outside. Still, on Christmas Eve, when it seemed as though every family was rejoicing, his heart ached.

Memories of those earlier Christmas Eves flooded in as he and Marcey entered the candle drenched church, drooping a bit with fatigue and disappointment. The prelude had already begun, an organ and piano version of "Greensleeves" that seemed more plaintive to him than joyful. Even seeing Bob Hamner greeting everyone in his red velvet jacket he wore only on Christmas Eve couldn't ignite the Christmas spark. Bob was generally rather dour, a quiet unassuming businessman who took a low profile in the church, but he insisted on being a greeter on Christmas Eve. Liberally fortified by Christmas spirits of several earlier parties, Bob was abnormally effusive, smiling broadly and hugging all the women.

There were only a few things about which Bob was passionate, but Christmas Eve was one of them. He had sternly lectured young Fred Backus in his first year as minister, "You must be sure that we're singing 'Silent Night' and lifting our candles precisely as midnight strikes. Finish too soon or too late and Christmas is ruined." Fred found himself madly signaling to the readers and organist to "slow it down" or "speed it up," cutting and adding verses of hymns with increasing intensity as that midnight deadline loomed. To ruin someone's Christmas because an *adagio* was taken too slowly was too much weight to bear.

Marcey seemed to settle into the service, singing the hymns with enthusiasm, if a little teary-eyed, but Keith only half-heard the lessons. The story was so familiar he slipped into auto-pilot as soon as they began. His minded drifted as he looked at the people around him. There were many unfamiliar faces, but also many who had played an important part in his life. He kept thinking how nice it would be if some day he could be there surrounded by his children and grandchildren. The Rinaldi family was all there, fourteen of them. Tony had been his best friend growing up. What fits they gave to Tony's mother Mildred, especially during the Christmas pageant that she always directed. One year the theme was based on the song "The Friendly Beasts," and she made them dress up with donkey ears and sing:

> "I," said the donkey all shaggy and brown,
> "I carried his mother up hill and down.
> I carried his mother to Bethlehem town,
> I," said the donkey, all shaggy and brown.
> — Traditional, public domain

"I was twelve years old." Keith smiled to himself. "Can you imagine the embarrassment?"

His eye caught Miss Isabel Snelling, who was still trying to lead the fifth-grade class through the escapades of Saul, David, and Solomon and make sense of God's faithfulness to a group of kids more interested in video games and soccer. "Ah, teaching Sunday school," his grandmother used to say, "It's like trying to herd cats." He had never given much thought to why Miss Snelling did it all those years. She was the last of her family, her older sister having died several years ago. Keith wondered what she did on Christmas with no family, and as he looked around realized there were others who didn't fit neatly into family groupings, for whom Christmas may have been a particularly lonely time.

Before he knew it, they were singing "Silent Night" and receding into the darkness with their candles. Greetings were exchanged with a number of friends. Even strangers on Christmas Eve were wont to say "Merry Christmas." Back in the car, Marcey commented, "Good message for us tonight, didn't you think?" "Mm" Keith mumbled, not wanting to admit he had hardly heard a word of the sermon.

As they pulled into the driveway they were surprised to see lights on in the house. "I'm sure I turned them off,"

Marcey said. They entered cautiously and were startled to discover that in their absence their barren home had been transformed. A fully decorated Christmas tree took its place of honor in the living room. Holly and ivy covered the mantelpiece. A crèche was set up on the marble top sideboard. Elves and Santas and angels were scattered in odd places and a sign announcing "Joy to the World" hung from the door. "The Little Drummer Boy" was playing on the CD and beside a plate of homemade cookies, a little note which read "A gift from your church family, to wish you a Merry Christmas and remind you that there is a light which continues to shine in the darkness." It was as if a pin pricked all their pent up emotions, and their wounds were drained.

Between laughter and tears, Keith and Marcey peppered each other with questions. Who might have done this? How did they get a key? Who didn't we see at the service? Who knew what we were going through and why Christmas might have been a little tough?

They began thinking about faith and family, their hungers and hopes, and the meaning of Christmas. They talked late into the night about deep things. Sometimes it seems as though we are without a home, without a family like other families. Jesus knew that — he entered this world a refugee, with no place to put his head except a manger. There was little conventional about his birth and his beginnings. He never married or had children. He never "fit." Yet wasn't it his mission, Marcey suggested, to help everyone else find their place, to know their home? Keith thought about all those people at church who had touched him through the years and those who had decorated their home. Aren't they our family, our real family, God's family? Single or married, widowed or divorced, childless or child-heavy, they are reminders that we have a home wherever God in Jesus Christ is present. We are family.

The incarnation is one of those great unexplainable mysteries. How is Jesus both God and human; how can a virgin be a mother; how can the majesty and might of God be encompassed in a human being? Theologians chew on these subjects and we know much from their speculations. But maybe, just maybe, we know the incarnation when we discover that Christ enters our world in ordinary ways, maybe even through some twinkling lights and ceramic angels put up by friends on a Christmas Eve when we were feeling low and even a little sorry for ourselves. God became incarnate for Keith and Marcey that night when they discovered they had a place they could always call home and a family which went beyond biology. It was a Christmas they would not soon forget.

Prayer

Out of the noise and glitter of the world's Christmas, we have come away, O God, into this hour in your presence. As Jesus came into the world, unexpectedly, surprisingly, never quite fitting, yet enabling others to find their place, help us to discover the home we have in God's family. Thank you for those who remind us of our place in the family of God, whatever our circumstance or situation in life. Help us to live as people who find our place at the manger and then carry this good news of great joy to all we see. In Jesus' name. Amen.

The Gift

It was a tradition he wished they could avoid, but in Sherry's family, it was inviolable. On Christmas Day the entire family gathered together and opened their gifts — one by one. That way, everyone got to see every gift, and what was more important, at least to some, the reaction as the presents were unveiled. The squeals of delight when the gift was clearly a winner, the halting efforts to find the right words and show the right expression, when the recipient wasn't quite sure what to make of it. "Will you look at this? How interesting! Who would have thought?"

Ken had to admit sometimes it was quite amusing. Sherry's brother Ben liked to keep a running tab as he compared the estimated value of the gifts he gave with those he received. And of course, he was always grumbling in mock horror as each gift was opened. "Another tie, when I gave you a dozen Strata golf balls. I've got to be $150 down by now," he'd complain. There was a lot of laughing, but sometimes Ken wondered if there might be a touch of seriousness to his economic calculations.

More than most, Ken understood the peculiar dynamics of gift giving. By the time Christmas came, Ken was always exhausted. He was the manager of the Claymoor's Department store out in the mall. He didn't have much patience with those who decried the commercialization of Christmas. Oh, he fully agreed that it was important to "keep Christ in Christmas" and to be sure folks knew "Jesus was the reason for the season." He was a regular at First Presbyterian, even served a term on Session. Occasionally some of the sales clerks would complain, especially about the last minute shoppers. "Look at these people. They're just buying anything. Don't they know that on December 26, we'll be the ones who will have to suffer when all those gifts are exchanged for something their friends really want?" It was natural to let off some steam, but Ken wouldn't put up with it for long. "If these people didn't buy — you wouldn't have a job." His success depended on the Christmas season.

But that didn't stop Ken — and Sherry too — from enjoying stories about misguided Christmas gifts. They remembered hearing Garrison Keillor tell of how he once received from a dear friend a Burgundy polo shirt for Christmas. He thanked him, and tried it on, but was thinking inside, "Burgundy? Burgundy shirts are worn by guys who smoke cigarillos, drive Buick LeSabres, sit in the dark corners of cocktail lounges, and place large wagers on basketball games." Keillor thought of himself as more of a "wheat" or "antique blue" kind of guy. So he put the burgundy shirt in a special corner of his closet with never-to-be-worn clothes. And after a three-month Christmas gift-cooling-off period required by law, he gave the shirt to a shelter for the homeless.

As they got ready to go off to the annual family gift exchange, Ken and Sherry were well aware that there was a peril to gifts — giving and receiving.

The family gathering went smoothly enough. It was always tough to get the children to be patient with this process when they wanted to rip open their presents in a semi-dazed frenzy common to most families. In Sherry's family — there were eighteen of them gathered — the process took a couple of hours. But the expected reactions occurred. There was much laughter and squeals of delight and, of course, some strained looks trying to conceal disappointment. They always worried about the children's reaction. They had the natural parental desire not to let their children down. It couldn't always be helped, however. Ken remembered a few years back when the Cabbage Patch® dolls were all the craze. Every year there was some item that just everyone *had* to have, and retailers like him went crazy trying to keep them in stock. The gimmick with the Cabbage Patch® dolls was that you just didn't buy one. You were adopting one, for a price of course, with her own special name. Melissa, their oldest child, nine at the time, claimed every girl she knew was getting a Cabbage Patch® for Christmas. Sherry had tried — she really had — but they were nowhere to be found. Several of her friends had traveled nearly a hundred miles away and waited in lines for up to two hours to get their Cabbage Patch®. One bought a doll over the internet at four times the price. "I'll be darned if I'm going to do that just so she won't be disappointed," Sherry said, "not for something that six months from now will be sitting unnoticed in the closet." But, of course, Melissa, was crestfallen, and it only made matters worse that her cousin Kim had opened hers with a shout of glee.

Sherry's parents had figured out a sure-fire way to dampen the disappointment. A few weeks before Christmas, they'd go shopping together. They'd each point out what they wanted, then would disappear while the other made the purchase. They'd go through the ruse of wrapping, but when the moment to open gifts came, there was no surprise. "A red blazer, in my size too — just what I wanted," Sherry's mom exclaimed to her family, so predictably. Sherry loved her parents, but thought that took all the magic and all the expectation out of gift giving. "I want you to use your imagination a bit," she instructed Ken. "Think what I'd enjoy... but let me tell you, if you give me pots and pans, when what I'd really like is something from Victoria's Secret — you're in big trouble."

There's the rub. Gifts may tell us very little about ourselves, but a great deal about whom the other person thinks we are or wants us to be. More than one child has opened what they hoped would be the latest Red Hot Chili Peppers or 'N Sync CD, only to discover it's Bach's *Brandenburg Concertos*, given by parents in the hope they will come to appreciate the gift they wanted them to want. Ken and Sherry still could not get over the gift they once received from their next-door neighbors, good friends, who they thought knew them well. On a trip back to their home in North Dakota they discovered a novelty artist whose specialty was making animals out of dried buffalo dung. The stuff was selling like hotcakes back there but Ken and Sherry could still remember the stunned feeling they had when they opened the gift that was neatly packaged and clearly identified as a "North Dakota Turd Bird." Their friends roared with delight, sure they had given the perfect gift, but Ken and Sherry were speechless. They had thought of themselves as cultured, sophisticated, the kind of people to whom you'd give a bottle of fine wine or the latest biography of John Adams, not a semi-crude joke gift.

Christmas is a holiday fraught with peril. Part of the peril of all this gift giving and gift getting is that we are stunned when we realize that somebody whom we love and who loves us, perceives us in a different way than we perceive ourselves. We don't always get what we expect.

The rest of the gift opening and the incredible dinner prepared by Sherry's mom left everyone stuffed. That was part of the tradition too. It was late by the time they left, but it had been a good Christmas. They drove home in relative quiet, listening to the one-day gift of Christmas music on the radio uninterrupted by commercials. But Ken was thinking a lot about gifts. We don't always get what we expect, he mused. He was thinking about his two teenage daughters in the backseat, so different in temperament, one quiet, tentative, introspective, the other fiery, opinionated, never uncertain about anything. Where did they come from, he thought to himself? Children are gifts from God, he often heard the preacher say. But he was thinking that sometimes in the gift of our children, God gives us gifts we might not have asked for, but which turn out so much better than what we might have imagined.

The strains of "O Little Town Of Bethlehem" were playing on the radio. He began to think of the great gift God gave us in Christmas. Unto us a child is born, unto us a son is given. All the songs he had been listening to were songs of joy, of gratitude and thanksgiving for this greatest of all gifts. But Ken thought to himself that Jesus wasn't always seen as a good gift. The way the Bible told it, Joseph was thrown into great consternation when he was told of the coming birth. Mary was greatly troubled when she realized that she was to have a child out of wedlock. When the angels announced the gift to the shepherds, the first words out of their mouths were "Fear not, for I bring you good news."

Jesus wasn't the gift people were expecting. They thought the messiah might come as a mighty military ruler to restore Israel's fortunes to their former glory. Others thought he might simply be a great spiritual leader, the kind who stuck to religion and stayed out of politics, someone who had sweet uplifting sayings that might help everyone better adjust to his situation in captivity.

But that wasn't the gift they received. Ken remembered the words from Handel's "Messiah," "And the government shall be upon his shoulders." He would rule, but not like earthly rulers, but as a servant. He would be the Prince of Peace, and yet would be a disturber of the status quo; one who would criticize the religious establishment and turn the values of the world upside down. This was the gift they got, the gift they needed, even though it was not necessarily the gift they wanted.

Gifts have a way of surprising us. Ken turned to Sherry, "I've been thinking," he said, "the real challenge of Christmas is not giving the right gift. It's being the kind of person that can receive a gift in the right way, even when it's not what was expected. That is what God is asking us to do, to receive the gift of Jesus, not because he proves to be what we expected. He almost always surprises us. We have to learn to receive the gift of Jesus, because he is the gift we most need."

Sherry just nodded; she was used to Ken's occasional philosophical reflections. Both got quiet again as the radio played a carol they had heard so many times before, yet never quite heard.

How silently, how silently, the wondrous gift is given
So God imparts to human hearts the blessings of his heaven
No ear may hear his coming, but in this world of sin
Where meek souls will receive him, still the dear Christ enters in.

Prayer

O God, giver of every good and perfect gift: You provide for us not so much what we want as what we need. You provide the gift of your Son Jesus, who brings us love and joy and hope. Help us this Christmas to be open to receiving that gift, and so receiving, offering the promise of "Emmanuel," God with us, your presence among us. For it is what the whole world most needs, not only at Christmas, but always. In Jesus' name. Amen.

Receiving at Christmas

"Helen must be wondering what happened to me," Henry Rifkin thought to himself as he collected the assorted floral tape, pruning shears, and other paraphernalia from the front pews. Each year the job of decorating the church for Christmas Eve seemed to take a little longer. He began sweeping up the spruce needles that had already fallen from the Chrismon tree. They seemed to get into everything, even onto the pews, and he didn't want anyone complaining they were being stuck in inopportune places as they settled into church that night.

Not that he minded this job that he and Helen had done for more than a dozen years at Central Presbyterian Church. It had been his long-standing custom to close the office down at noon on Christmas Eve, meet his wife for lunch, and then get to work, setting up the tree, placing the poinsettias, wrapping the pine rope around the chancel rail, arranging the white and red carnations in the memorial vases. Helen was the creative one, of course, having learned this fine art from her mother, the "grand dame of church floral decorating." It amazed him that each year she came up with new ideas, variations on a theme, of course, but different enough to capture people's attention. Henry knew his job was simply to follow her orders, moving ladders, cutting evergreens, positioning and repositioning the flowers until everything was just right.

It was tradition in the congregation that the sanctuary never be decorated before Christmas Eve. One year, when the children were smaller, they proposed decorating the Sunday before Christmas Eve. It certainly would have made preparations in their household easier. The worship committee in classic Presbyterian fashion debated it for thirty minutes before Artura Dalrymple, pronounced the definitive word. "People have to walk in on Christmas Eve and know that it's different than any other time, special, unique, magical. That's why we never decorate before Christmas Eve at Central." And that was that. The Rifkins learned there was no point tampering with some traditions.

Their work largely done, Henry sent Helen home to get ready for their own Christmas Eve, while he remained to finish up. He loved how the dying sun made the ochre and cobalt blues of the stained-glass windows look so rich. He loved the emptiness of the building — ministers and musicians having gone home for a brief respite before the flood of services began. It was a perfect time to do some quiet reflection on his life, which he was prone to do at this time of the year.

In a way it was surprising he had become so active in church. His own upbringing had trained him to be rather indifferent about the whole enterprise. As the youngest of four, he had shaped his attitude toward the big issues of life by watching others. When his oldest brother was killed in an automobile accident coming home from a year's duty in Vietnam, something in his father snapped. "How could God do this to me?" he railed, "He emerged unscathed from war, only to be killed because someone ran a light?" Soon his father's anger degenerated into a general sourness. He wouldn't even let the family celebrate holidays and birthdays anymore. "I lost a son too," his mother gently reminded her husband. "We don't all have to be punished." But his father did not relent. In his bitterness, he was determined to make everyone unhappy. His mother was a saint, hurting too, but handling it differently. She'd occasionally try to pry open faith for the family, but his father's favored response to anything remotely churchy, was "That's poppycock."

Henry, as teenage boys tend to do, followed his father's example more than his mother's words, when it came to religion. He saw no need to become bitter but neither did he find faith necessary or attractive. At least until he met Helen. Her patient, gentle faith had gradually drawn him in. For a few years of their married life he spent Sunday mornings playing golf or doing yard work. Going off to church, she'd needle him a bit, "Don't think you can get away that easy. You've been baptized. God's already got his hooks on you." That strange sacramental logic was lost on him, but she did not nag, and after a while, when the kids were born, he thought it good if he went occasionally. Before long, he found, to his surprise, that Helen was right. God did have his hooks on him. And it was good.

His reverie was interrupted by a sharp rap at the side door of the church. No one ever used that door, he thought, as he pulled it open. He could see in the shadows a disheveled looking couple, a pale complexioned girl not more than eighteen or nineteen, in tattered jeans, with carrot red hair pulled back, and piercings in places that looked like they really hurt. There was with her a guy, somewhat older, with full beard, rough hewn, unkempt, dressed in a grease-stained jacket and frayed working boots. Henry could make out a ring of tattoos around his neck, and only wondered where else they might be. He guessed they hadn't arrived early for the 7 p.m. carol service.

"Mister," the tattooed man croaked. "Can you help us? We're trying to get to Bethel Corners and our car is giving us trouble. We're nearly out of money. Can you find a place for us to stay?"

Henry winced. He didn't like this. It was one thing to work the Salvation Army kettle with other Rotarians. That was kind of fun. But to get involved with these kind of people was something else. He caught himself and felt a little shame for his judgmentalism, but still, where was the minister when you really needed her?

Henry found all his suspicions surfacing. Didn't his father, whenever he thought charity encouraged sloth, which in his opinion was most of the time, always say, "I believe what the Bible says: God helps those who help themselves." Henry had long since realized that quote wasn't in the Bible, but still, questions peppered his mind. "How could you get caught on a trip without any money? How do I know you're not lying and are just looking to buy drugs? Why didn't you go to the rescue shelter? Do you care anything about the church or are you just using it?" His mind wavered precariously on that delicate edge between cynicism and sentiment, between wanting to help, especially on Christmas Eve, and a natural desire to take seriously a real biblical admonition "to be wise as a serpent," especially when it came to money.

Almost as if she could read his thoughts, the woman spoke up, "Really mister, it's not what you think. It's not just a scam to get money and avoid honest work."

"Well, that had crossed my mind," Henry was thinking.

"Don't think this comes easy to us." she went on. "We've been living down in Birkhead, had various jobs, but got ourselves overextended. And yeah, we did more than our share of partying. My boyfriend here thought he had a good job lined up, but then it fell through and we decided we'd had enough. We're lonely and at least in Bethel City we have some kin. We're hoping to have a baby real soon, but it seems things just haven't gone right. We stopped last night in a shelter and had some of our stuff stolen. We just do not want to do that again. Now the car is acting up. Can't you help us?" Her candor was disarming and began to erode his defenses.

It was a good story, maybe too good. He remembered the minister telling them she had heard so many hard luck stories and listened to so many people swear they would return the money when they got back on their feet, without it having happened even once, that it was hard not to be cynical. One time after meeting with three or four folks whose stories just got more and more outlandish, she finally said to the last guy, "I'm afraid I just don't buy your story. Can't you come up with something better than that?" Undaunted, the man responded, "Well how about this one?" and began to weave a new fantasy as if the quality of the story would determine the size of the handout.

Henry had all the reasons for sending the couple on their way, and maybe it was the triumph of sentiment over cynicism, maybe it was their desire to have a baby that tugged on his heart, and maybe it was the thought of another unwed couple 2,000 years ago, and his realization that if someone hadn't taken a chance on them, and maybe risked being duped, Mary and Joseph wouldn't have had even a stable for their boy — maybe it was all of those things, but he could not let them go. Henry could hear the choir beginning to gather at the other end of the building. Time was growing short. Whether on impulse or instruction of the Holy Spirit, he said, "Hey, tell you what. Help me get this place cleaned up, and we'll see what we can do."

And so for the next half hour they swept and carried out discarded cuttings and wiped up the dirt spills so that everything would be just right. Henry found out a lot about them — and how difficult their life had been. Shelly jumped at the first opportunity to get away from her abusive and alcoholic father. Mike had been in several foster homes, dropped out of high school, and with no skills to his name had bounced from job to job. Their neediness had drawn them together, and they said they really loved each other, but neither had known much of a model of love in growing up. Being a Presbyterian, evangelism did not come easy to Henry, but since it was Christmas Eve, it did not seem too unnatural to ask them about whether they ever went to church or had a faith which helped them. "When you've had a life like mine," Mike responded, "you figure this notion that there is someone out there to help you is pretty much poppycock." Henry was startled that he used that same word as his father, but noticed that nevertheless they had known enough about church to seek it out as a place of help.

It was close to service time, Henry made a quick call to explain to Helen not to wait, he would join the family at church. He threw his tools into his car, they got into theirs, which sputtered quite a bit before it got moving. They stopped at a Waffle House where they were the only customers, the three of them eating largely in silence, looking like a scene from an Edward Hopper painting. Henry found a budget motel on the far side of town, clean but simple, and paid for the room. He invited them to church, but they declined. It was a reminder that in life, unlike the movies, compassion does not easily produce Christmas Eve conversions. Still it felt good when Mike said to him, "God bless you mister, maybe we'll see you again."

Henry actually hoped they would. He hurried back to church and nestled into his seat beside Helen and the kids just as the choir was singing his favorite line from "O Little Town of Bethlehem," "Yet in the dark streets shineth, the everlasting light. The hopes and fears of all the years are met in thee tonight." Somehow it seemed a bit truer this year.

Prayer

Comfort giving God: On Christmas we marvel once again with the miracle of new birth. You come down to us, incarnate in a baby, who grows up to show us how to live, to have life abundantly and to know life eternal. As you came into a strange place and were welcomed, so challenge us to welcome strangers into our midst, and be ambassadors of your care and compassion. In Jesus' name we pray. Amen.

The Christmas Peace

It was a tradition he did not like, but could not avoid. Paul Hawkins was valiantly trying to pull his two children away from their toys and into the car for the annual Christmas Day gathering at Uncle Harry's and Aunt Martha's.

Once, when the children were young he tried to beg off, saying it was too much to drive two hours and then return so late. But his parents would not hear of it. "Everyone will be there and it's the least you could do to be part of this family," his mother had told him. That was the problem. Everyone *would* be there — his parents, sister and brother, several cousins, and their assorted children — 29 in all. There was hardly room to breathe.

It wasn't just the chaos. It was the dynamics. His aunt had a sign in her kitchen, "We're the family that puts the fun in dysfunctional." The dysfunctional part he understood, but these gatherings were anything but fun. He had read the polls that said family time, not the birth of Jesus, was the most important part of Christmas — 44 to 33%. That always evokes a lot of clerical hand wringing, pulpit jeremiads "that Christ had been evacuated from Christmas." Mercifully his minister had not gone that way in his Christmas Eve sermon.

Still, Paul wondered who these families were that loved "family time." "Do we have to go?" Sarah and Henry were whining as they got into the car.

Like most people, he wished his Christmas could be peaceful like a Thomas Kincaid painting, harmonious, uncluttered by conflict, calm. When he expressed this yearning to someone at work, he was surprised by her response. "Did you ever notice that there are hardly any people in Kincaid's paintings? People and peace don't seem to go together," she said.

As he pulled onto the highway he thought back to that moment when these gatherings had begun to degenerate. He called it the "Great Regifting Fiasco" of 1999. Even Dr. Phil now has ethics experts on his show talking about the acceptability of regifting — but then it was morally suspect. "Do you remember it?" he said to his wife Karen, "how my sister gave us the cheese board she had gotten from Martha and Harry the year before? If they thought they put one over on us, they were mistaken. And to think, we had given her a new David Winter cottage — cost us $56." "Remember it?" Karen said, "How could I forget it? You told your sister she was a cheapskate. Then others admitted they had regifted too, and before we knew it the whole crowd was taking up sides. It was horrible. Don't you think it is time to just let it go?" She was right, of course, but it just burned him.

He thought back to the Christmas Eve service the night before and how peaceful it had made him feel. The choir soared when it sang those words "peace on earth, good will toward all." Why is it so hard to keep that mood even for 24 hours? He spotted Lillian Wakefield's son Michael who had just completed a tour of duty in Afghanistan and was now home on leave, and thought about all those who were in harm's way, in places in the world that were anything but peaceful. He had learned a disturbing fact back in college that since the coming of the Prince of Peace, there had only been 37 years in human history free of fighting somewhere. He loved the story of how on Christmas 1914, in the middle of WW I, peace had broken out in the trenches. It started with the British singing carols and the Germans' responding. A truce was arranged, and the opposing armies, which had shot at each other just days before, met in the "no-man's land," that hundred yards separating the forces. They exchanged gifts, shared cups of coffee, and held a service for their fallen dead. When they returned to their trenches a lone voice began singing "Silent Night," and soon all joined in, each singing the familiar carol in his own language. That's what should happen on Christmas, he thought.

They finally arrived. They had come the farthest and were the last there. The activity was in full swing — the exchange of gifts, drinks and hor d'oevres abounding, animated conversations all around. There were the obligatory words about how disappointed they were that Marcy, Paul's cousin, had chosen to spend the day with her in-laws. But frankly, she never felt at home with the rest of them. It wasn't long before his brother Stuart, though divorced for eight years, started complaining — again — about his ex-wife, how upset he was about his kids being exposed to her new live-in boyfriend, and how inconsiderate she is about getting the kids to him on time on the holidays. "You think he'd be adjusting by now," Karen whispered to Paul. They both felt for Stuart's children Mark and Missy, who were never supposed to have much fun when they were with their mother, out of loyalty to their dad.

The dinner was fabulous, as always — roast turkey with chestnut stuffing and cranberries. Whatever else, it was a family of good cooks. Plenty of mashed potatoes for the kids, Martha's famous spinach soufflé, a superb tomato cheese casserole, pineapple stuffing (the specialty of cousin Richard), pumpkin pie for dessert. The table extended all the way through the dining room into the living room — and there was room for everyone. The children asked to be excused, and before long they were in heated play, with arguments about whose turn it was to use the play station, and the sound of transformers being crashed against each other in mock battle providing a counterpoint to the adult conversation.

Paul, as he always did, begged Karen on the ride over, not to get drawn into conversations about religion or politics, but it was futile. She couldn't resist herself. Uncle Harry, lubricated by too much wine, got on his soapbox about religion being intolerant and the root cause of conflict. Before long opinions about the war in Iraq and President Bush were flying around the table. "He started the war on false pretense." "So you'd have him sit back and do nothing? Don't you realize 9/11 changed everything?" "We have to let the Iraqis take over. Our presence is only making things worse." "So are you just going to cut and run?" "My friend just got back and said things are a lot better than the press suggests. They're always negative." Before long voices were raised and degenerated into less than helpful commentary. "Well you're just stupid." "You'd vote for the devil if he were on the Republican ticket." "At least I'm not a tax and spend liberal." Words were hurled around the room like weapons of mass destruction, which in a sense they were. Everyone was in on it, except cousin Catherine. She sat like a great stone Buddha, finding her own peace by pretending none of this was happening.

There seemed little prospect of ending the fracas. Then someone noticed that seven year old Emily, a refugee from the children's room, had positioned herself next to the wall and had her hands covering her ears. "What's the matter, Emily?" her mother finally said.

Slowly Emily uncovered her ears; her face was etched with a sadness which made her look older than her years. "It's Christmas, people. It's Jesus' birthday. We learned in Sunday school he came to bring peace. So why are all the kids fighting and all of you in this room yelling?"

Paul's mother tried to rush to the rescue, "We're not yelling, we're discussing," she said, but they all knew Emily was right.

You could hear a pin drop. People sat in stunned silence. "Out of the mouths of babes," someone finally said. It wasn't that Emily's words turned their Christmas around. That would overstate it. But perhaps it made them a bit more attentive to remembering the presence of the one who was the source of all the celebration.

As Paul drove home that night the car was strangely silent, everyone having been exhausted by the events of the day. Paul thought to himself, "How elusive peace is." Though he came as Prince of Peace, Jesus himself became the occasion for Herod's raging and the slaughter of the innocents. Mary was told by Simeon when she presented Jesus in the temple that he would evoke opposition, and "a sword would pierce her own soul."

The Bible gives little evidence that peace will cover up the world's conflicts or mask much of the human pain.

Paul listened more intently as the radio played Henry Wadsworth Longfellow's familiar carol:

> I heard the bells on Christmas day their old familiar carols play,
> And wild and sweet the words repeat of peace on earth good will to men.
> And in despair I bowed my head, "there is no peace on earth," I said.
> For hate is strong and mocks the song of peace on earth, good will to men.

Though it seems that way sometimes, there is something else, a peace of God which passes all understanding, which surprises us and keeps breaking into our world giving us hints of another reality, another truth, signs of a coming kingdom.

It had been a good Christmas all in all — and Paul realized that even within his family, he could, by grace, discover something of God's peace. As he drifted off to sleep the little sung last verse ran through his head.

> Then pealed the bells more loud and deep: God is not dead, nor does he sleep.
> The wrong shall fail, the right prevail, with peace on earth good will to men.

Prayer

Loving God, you came to earth as the Prince of Peace, but peace remains so elusive. Our fears lead us to mistrust those different than we are, our greed makes us covet what we do not need, our pride makes it difficult for us to admit when we are wrong. Conflict takes control, where peace should reign. Forgive our severing ways, O Lord, and by your presence let reconciliation triumph. In Jesus' name. Amen.

Pondering Christmas

It was going to be a different Christmas this year, Billy Hardesty thought to himself as he herded his young family into the car. The day after Christmas for every one of his 28 years, he had gone to the Hardesty family homestead in Southside, Virginia. Christmas itself was always at home but the day after belonged to his grandparents. It took a little negotiating with Catherine after he got married to see whose family got which holiday, and he was relieved when she consented to this yearly pilgrimage.

This year would be different. Eighty-seven-year-old Madolin, the matriarch and family glue, had died in August following a short illness. Uncle Bucky and Aunt Helen thought it wise to change the tradition and have the gathering at their house, but Grandpa would have none of it. "Christmas will be here — and that's the end of the discussion," he said — and it was.

Billy was glad, and yet he still wondered what it would be like. Holidays can be blue times for those who have suffered loss, and Christmas is often marked more by who isn't at the table than who is. He had never experienced the death of a close relative before, and his grandmother's absence at the table would certainly be a powerful presence. Indeed, Madolin Hardesty was always a powerful presence, energetic, boisterous, compassionate, strong-willed, plain spoken, slightly irreverent. "Your grandmother is one of a kind," Henry Hardesty would say. Billy's Dad put it differently, "My mother is a piece of work." Billy loved her just the way she was.

She did have a way of making everyone's business her business in a way that didn't always endear her to others. It was just that she was just so invested in everyone, so determined to hold everyone together. As was said of Theodore Roosevelt, she was one of those people who wanted to be the bride at every wedding, the baby at every baptism, and the corpse at every funeral.

Who could forget that 85th birthday when she stood up in that bright purple dress, read the poem "When I am old, I will wear purple," then put her hands on her hips and announced, "I may be old, but I'm not dead yet." You had to admire her spunk.

She could be a bit prickly. She loved singing "O Holy Night" in choir every Christmas, and no one dared to tell her she wasn't really hitting the high notes any more. But she was also funny and mercifully understanding of children. Once, when a family wedding seemed interminable, she grabbed Billy by the arm, and said, "Let's get out of here. I'm tired of being charming."

It was a relief to Billy when he entered the house and saw the styrofoam Santas and reindeer. He was glad his grandfather, who always deferred to Madolin in the Christmas decorating department had put them out. They were the product of his first venture into sales. His older brother Pete had to sell five as a fund-raising project for student council. Too busy or too embarrassed to take on the task, he promised Billy 25 cents for every one he sold. When he told people his brother was making him sell what he now knew were the tackiest of decorations, he got plenty of sympathy — and sales. Pete was none too happy to learn his little brother had not only sold what was required but took orders. He had to shell out $5 in commission — big money in those days. His grandmother bought two Santas and five reindeer and put them out every Christmas. Billy expected it. Children, whatever their age, are the most ruthless preservers of Christmas tradition.

Grandma Hardesty knew how to celebrate Christmas — the decorations, the food, the presents. There was always a big pile of presents. Billy suspected his two grandmothers were in a bit of competition but he didn't mind that orgy of indulgence. Wasn't the competitive spirit the American way — especially if it worked to his advantage? If Billy grew up knowing Christmas was more than that, it was primarily because of his grandmother. Gift opening always began with her reminder that we give gifts because God has given so much to us. And there were "Jesus is the reason for the season" reminders in nearly every room.

By 4 p.m., the family had gathered. There was lots of animated conversation around the living room as the gifts were being opened and snacks served and it wasn't all edifying. There was the usual grumbling about immigration policy and all the undocumented workers who were coming to the free medical clinic, and the problems with the Arabs, and how the Chinese were poised to take over our economy. "Every Christmas decoration I bought was made in China," Billy's cousin Francine complained. None of the Hardesty clan would have viewed themselves as prejudiced, but sometimes it was hard to tell.

Finally it was time for the seventeen of them to gather at the table. There was an awkward silence as they wondered who would ask the blessing. That was Grandma Madolin's job. She never quite trusted Henry to do it right but tonight he stepped in and it turned out Henry Hardesty offered quite a fine prayer — and the dinner was launched.

That unspoken memory around the table unleashed a mealtime's worth of conversation about the one who was absent. Everyone had a story about Madolin and Billy was happy to share some of his favorites.

Growing up, Billy wasn't much of a churchgoer because his parents weren't, but he always attended the little Highbridge Presbyterian Church when he visited the family homestead. He knew God meant something to his grandparents and they always took time to answer his questions.

When his grandmother came to see him play basketball, he asked her about the practice of his Catholic friends to cross themselves before a foul shot. "What good does that do?" "Not much," his grandmother replied, "unless they know how to play basketball!"

When he was about ten, Tyrone, one of his friends from the basketball team asked him to sleep over on Saturday and go with him to Mount Olive AME church the next day. It was right before Christmas, and the church already had a manger scene set up in the sanctuary. It startled Billy because the baby in the manger was black. It was the first time he realized not everyone pictured Jesus in the same way. On the Christmas visit that year he asked his grandmother about it. "Billy, there aren't any pictures of Jesus. And I think God meant it that way. He was Palestinian and probably had a swarthy, olive complexion, with dark eyes and black hair. He probably wasn't anything like the blond-haired blue-eyed picture of Jesus I stared at in my Sunday school room as a girl. But it doesn't matter. When we look at Jesus, we see ourselves in a mirror, we see him as one of us, who knows, understands, and relates to us as we are. But likewise, he's one of them, knowing, loving, and understanding others, who may not look like us."

Billy told how she broke into a song that he had never heard, but he had now taught his children: *Jesus loves the little children, all the children of the world; red and yellow, black and white, they are precious in his sight. Jesus loves the little children of the world.* He remembered how excited his grandmother was when Uncle Bob and Aunt Ruth adopted a child from China. That year she put up a crèche where all the figures looked Asian.

"Billy you have to ponder Jesus — like Mary — and think about who this Jesus is, and how he's not just for us, but for all the peoples of the world."

As a child you don't do much pondering, but as you grow older, pondering, thinking, trying to understand, becomes part of life. Mary, a new, young, and still unmarried mother, was undoubtedly overwhelmed by a visit from those roughhewn shepherds, who told her strange tales of an angelic chorus and brought back her own experience of an angel visitation. Mary had good reason to "ponder all this in her heart," as the gospel says. Mary would come to know that her child, though hers, was not just hers, but belonged to all the people.

As he left his grandfather's home that night, and Billy pondered the conversation around the table, he realized it had been a good Christmas. His grandmother was gone but had been very present that night in reminding them all of God's presence. So often we come to Christmas having created our own image of who this Jesus is. His grandmother, even from the grave, had reminded him once again of that promise of Jesus, 2,000 years old and yet still unfulfilled, that we can transcend our differences and find our peace and our unity in the family of God, where all the barriers we set up are all broken down.

Prayer

At Christmastime, we are reminded of those special people in our lives who have gone before us and who told us the good news about Jesus. We thank you that Jesus is no provincial deity, a god made in our image, but rather a Lord who seeks to remake us in his image. Remind us this night that Jesus transcends all our differences and loves all the children of the world, red, yellow, black, or white, who see him through the eyes of their own culture. In his name we pray. Amen.

Grabbed by Grace

It was already snowing hard when the office closed at noon, and Jeff Rendell had heard they were closing the airports. So perhaps it was just as well he had decided to stay in the city for Christmas. His family in Kokomo was disappointed, but he couldn't justify spending $430 to get home for two days. And he wasn't all that eager to have to endure the family questions, "What's going on at work? Are you paying your bills on time? What about that girl you were dating? Isn't it about time to settle down and get married? Are you going to church?" And yet, there was still a certain longing. "Man, do I miss those school vacations," the 27-year-old account executive thought to himself. "This working world is not all it's cracked up to be."

Actually he liked his job well enough. It had been his dream to work in New York, and here he was in the Big Apple, making more money just four years out of college than his parents were making with thirty years of experience. But still, his rent was so expensive; he barely felt he was keeping his head above water. There was not a whole lot of spare cash to enjoy the theater or a dinner at Ruth Chris' steakhouse.

Despite its image as a source of perpetual fun for a young single guy, New York could also be rather lonely. Most of his friends were going to be with family, so Jeff was feeling rather melancholy as he walked down Eighth Avenue.

He stepped into the Old World Café, although there wasn't much old world about its cafeteria style dining, other than the occasional *sauerbraten* on the menu. He ordered meat loaf, and the server, none too happy to be working on Christmas Eve, barked at him "mashed potatoes"? He nodded gently, and she splattered them on his plate with a thud, and shouted "next," deepening his funk. "Christmas Eve has come to this?" Jeff wondered.

Emerging from the restaurant buoyed by meat and mashed potatoes — his version of comfort food, Jeff pulled down his hat, and tightened his jacket against the weather, as he thought of Christmases past. His reverie was broken by the ringing of his cell phone. It was playing "Frosty the Snowman" in honor of the season. Laughter erupted from the phone with the caller obviously trying to get control of himself. "Jeff, it's Ronnie. Whassup?" Ronnie was Ronnie Evans, his best friend from Kokomo, who having been married just six months ago, was presumably more mature, though you couldn't tell it from his tone. "The guys are all here — and guess what we're talking about?" Ronnie had returned to Kokomo after college to work in his father's electronics business, but the others — Bud Nichols, Hank Haspell, and Nicky Farintino — unmarried like him were home for the holidays and were gathering to tell tales.

"Remember that little episode when we were all seniors?" Jeff remembered all right. They were all home from college, complaining that there was nothing to do in this boring town. He couldn't remember whose idea it was, but he was the perpetrator. Right next to the town center, in front of the Anderson insurance agency, was a life-size manger scene sponsored by the Exchange Club. When such displays were banned on the town green, Ed Anderson, President of the Exchange, announced, "I'm not going to let political correctness prevent me from proclaiming my faith." On that night, as they drove by the agency, someone, emboldened by an ample quantity of Bud light, which had been consumed by everyone except the designated driver, shouted, "Hey, let's take baby Jesus out for a drink." The car screeched to a halt, Jeff had jumped out, grabbed the baby Jesus, and they went off to Applebee's Bar and Grill, where they propped up the figurine and were having a good old time. The Applebee's hostess was not amused, however, by their amusement and bad taste and called the police.

The officer gave them a stern tongue-lashing, made them return to the scene of the crime, and apologize. The local paper had fun with a front-page story, "college guys abduct Jesus" with a picture of the policeman returning the stolen goods. Mr. Anderson, contacted by the paper, explained, "The other figurines in the nativity scene are wired down, but we can't really tie down the baby Jesus."

That comment struck Jeff as odd, because of course, you could — with ingenuity, strong wire, determination, and lots of twisting and wrapping, you certainly could tie Jesus down.

Ronnie's call lifted Jeff's spirits. It was embarrassing at the time, one of those lapses of judgments for which students are famous, but with the passing of time the great Jesus grab seemed hilarious again.

He hadn't meant to be sacrilegious; he had done obligatory penance in Sunday school and respected the good people in Trinity Presbyterian Church. But it had been some years since he had warmed any church pew. He wasn't hostile; it was just that he felt he had outgrown any need for religion or faith. His life was filled with work, school, parties, dates, computer games, sports, music, TV shows, and friends. He wondered why religion seemed important to so many people.

Wandering aimlessly — he wasn't ready to go to an empty apartment just yet — and thinking about where his faith had gone — Jeff passed by a small brownstone church, looking well worn and neglected, not like those big elegant Fifth Avenue Gothic churches, Saint Thomas' and Saint Patrick's. "Christmas Eve dinner served here — all welcome," the signpost announced, Jeff impulsively went in to see if he could help. Volunteers were scurrying everywhere, and when he finally figured out who was in charge — no easy task if you know the church — he learned that yes, some of their regulars hadn't been able to get in because of the snow, and they could use the help.

In an act of poetic justice, he was assigned the mashed potato detail, and in the midst of all the peeling, cutting, mashing, seasoning, and serving he was determined to bring an aura of dignity, warmth, grace, and compassion to the task unlike what he had experienced a few hours before.

It felt good for him to focus on something beyond himself for a while, and he was quite taken by the guests who started to arrive — wondering about their background and their lives. Some from the neighborhood were just lonely and didn't want to spend the time by themselves; some were breadwinners who had lost their jobs and were facing grinding poverty they had never known before. Some clearly had rather severe mental and emotional problems. They were probably off their meds and were showing the effects.

Jeff was struck by one man with baggy pants, a dirty shirt, and three day's growth of graying beard. His tuberous nose glowed hardly less than Rudolph's. His hair was unwashed and unkempt, and his toes were poking through his would-be shoes. He looked old, but his age was undeterminable, undoubtedly reflecting the ravages of alcohol and hard living.

He sat down with his food across the table from a young mother and her year-old baby, Erik. She was waiting for her husband to finish his volunteer shift. The old man began flapping his wrists, waving at Erik, "Hi there, baby; hi there, big boy; I see you, buster," Erik non-plussed, laughed and giggled. His mother looked a little uncomfortable as the man continued loudly, "Do you know patty cake? Do you know peek-a-boo? Hey everyone, he knows peek-a-boo." No one thought the man was cute; he obviously was drunk.

Except for Erik, who continued to show off his antics for the man, while his mother looked uncertain what to do. Erik, seemingly fascinated with the man, opened his arms in a baby's "pick me up" position. And before the mother could stop him, Erik had propelled himself to the man, who hugged him tightly. Everyone in the church hall froze, not sure what to do, but Jeff could see that the man's aged hands, caked in grime and pain, were gently stroking the baby's back. His eyes were closed and there were tears beneath his lashes. It seemed like an eternity, but then the man opened his eyes, fixed his gaze on the mother and said, "You take care of this baby." You could hear the catch in her voice as she stammered, "I will."

The old man pried Erik from his chest, lovingly and long-ingly as though he were in pain. "God, bless you ma'am. You've given me my Christmas gift," he said, and walked out into the storm.

Jeff stood there stunned, grabbed unexpectedly by God's grace. Ready to judge the man as simply a sad wreck of hu-manity, he could not have been more surprised to feel God's presence in that encounter, to see signs of God's love in the brokenness in a way that had long eluded him. Old Ed An-derson had been right, "You cannot tie Jesus down." Much as we do our best to keep him in the manger, sweet but in-nocuous, much as we want him in our control, unthreatening and unchallenging, Jesus has a way of bursting out. Some-how, sometime, perhaps on Christmas Eve, perhaps when you least expect it, Jesus can touch the core of your being, and everything looks different.

They finished serving the dinner, and Jeff decided to go upstairs for the Christmas Eve service — the first time he had been to worship since last Christmas. But it felt different when he sang, "How silently, how silently, the wondrous gift is given. So God imparts to human hearts, the blessings of his heaven."

When he left church, there was nearly ten inches of snow on the ground. As he trudged his way to the subway. He got on his cell phone and called home. His mother answered. "I love you, Mom, Merry Christmas," was all he said before he choked up in tears.

Prayer

O God of stars and stables, God of angels and shepherds, we praise you for the surprising grace we see not only in the birth of Jesus, but in his unexpected presence throughout each day. Give us eyes to see where you dwell. Give us hearts filled with your love, that we may be children of light. Give us tongues ready to sing of your joy come to the world. We pray in the name of the one who was born in Bethlehem, Jesus our redeemer. Amen.

The Invitation

She could feel her face becoming flush with embarrassment as she pushed open the door to the Salvation Army headquarters two weeks before Christmas and saw the motley looking crowd waiting in line. This wasn't a familiar setting for Carol Enwright, but she was feeling desperate. It had been three months since she lost her job in the office at Southside Ford. "Nothing personal," the manager had said, "but we're just not selling cars and we need to cut back." She understood; she had seen the figures, but it didn't make it any easier as a single parent just barely making it as it was.

It was tough enough to go to the unemployment office each week but that was nothing compared to the internal struggle she had put herself through before walking through that door to sign up for the turkey dinner and toy giveaway. "I'm just not the kind of person who takes charity." Carol said, "I'm the person who should be giving out the turkeys." She couldn't shake the comments she had heard friends make when they would read in the paper that 700 turkeys were needed this year. "Who in the world *are* all these people? Maybe they're spending their money foolishly. They could be working at McDonald's you know." Carol had to admit that sometimes those thoughts had crossed her mind, but the last months had shown her it was all too easy to get into a financial fix. It had been a struggle ever since Bill left her and her daughter Melissa for a younger woman two years ago. The money he provided for child support didn't begin to cover the expenses, and it was erratic.

Carol kept her head down, talked to no one in the line, answered the interviewer's questions perfunctorily, and got out of the Salvation Army headquarters as quickly as she could, hoping no one she knew had seen her.

Sleeting rain had begun to fall. She tightened her coat and walked more briskly toward her apartment. She wondered whether she should have responded more positively when her sister had called to invite them to come for Christmas. Melissa would have been happy to be there, to see her cousins and enjoy the elegant surroundings and fine cuisine. But not Carol.

Carol loved her older sister Sandy. She just couldn't be in the same room with her for more than five minutes without bickering. Holidays, she reasoned, always seem to bring out the worst in family dysfunction. Even as a child, Sandy was the favored one, the one who never gave their parents any trouble, the one who excelled in school. She had married the perfect husband, kept the perfect house, raised the perfect children — or so it seemed. It was just too much sometimes. Carol had always been a bit of a rebel, the one who didn't like to color in the lines, and the one who lived on the edge. Her sister warned her about marrying Bill. "Bill, you'll find, is all about Bill." Carol tried hard to make it work, but when Bill's infidelities became obvious, she decided enough was enough. She felt the unspoken judgment of her sister, "I told you so."

Since the last holiday gathering they had barely spoken. Especially since life had taken a turn for the worse, she didn't think she could take being with her.

Carol hadn't been very cordial when Sandy called to invite them for Christmas. She wanted to let rip the sarcastic response that was in her head. "Oh, you want to show off your fourteen foot impeccably decorated Blue Spruce tree, the Lennox china, that magnificent Dickens village you have set up in the den, and then wow us with your oyster stuffing and a $50 bottle of imported French wine." She wanted to say that but didn't, saying simply, "We're not sure what our plans for the day are."

Carol was glad to get out of the cold and back to the apartment. She put on some Christmas music, made herself a cup of tea, and was feeling quite sorry for herself as she settled down to open the Christmas greetings that had come in the mail that day. She opened up a card from David Wilson, who had been part of the church youth group growing up and who always made her laugh. Memories of Christmas pageants came flooding to her mind. There was the year Mrs. Spriggs decided to update the story. "Let's make it real," she said. They had played the holy couple driving home to Bethlehem in an old beat up Studebaker, that ran out of gas (it was 1974, the year of the first gas shortage) and Mary had to give birth in a seedy looking service station. Of course, the congregation hated it and the next year tradition returned. Another year David was the innkeeper. As a thirteen-year-old he had aspirations of being an actor and was going to play this bit part for all it was worth. When Mary and Joseph knocked, he opened the door and said with great gusto, "No, there's no room in the inn." But as he slammed the door shut he managed to pull the entire set down on top of him. After the clatter settled you could hear this little squeaky voice mutter, "Damn it, I'm so humiliated," to the congregation's great amusement. David was mortified, probably as much by the fact that he'd now have to answer to his mother for having sworn in church, as by the fact that the production was ruined. Actually it wasn't really ruined, it simply made it one of the most memorable pageants the church had ever known.

Carol opened a card from Helen Hocksley, an older woman who had mentored her in her first job out of college. The card included her usual, lengthy, three-page Christmas letter. Some Christmas letters are little more than a list of self-congratulatory achievements. Everything is beautiful in my life, darling. What about you? Carol wasn't eager to read many of those this year. But on the other hand, she didn't relish those letters which were little more than a litany of complaints, and that was usually Helen's. "In January, I broke my ankle and was laid up for six weeks. February we had a leak and the new roof cost us $10,000. In March Joey and Francine got divorced." And on it went through the year, until Carol cried out loud, "Helen, get over it!" But she was stopped short by the last paragraph, which said "At the end of November, my beloved Harry, my husband of 33 years, died suddenly. I know he is with the Lord, but you cannot imagine how much I'll miss him. Have a merry Christmas, Helen."

It was strange how something like that pulled Carol out of her self-pity into a more reflective mode. How fragile life is, she thought. Those we spend our lives loving or hating come and go so quickly. The last few months she hadn't been going to church much; maybe she was angry because God hadn't spared her these troubles. But as she listened to Christmas music, she started to hear its message and mull over what her relationships with family and friends meant to her, messy as they might be.

So she was ready to think differently when she opened the next card. It was one of those musical cards, which started playing "Santa Baby" with its conspicuous consumption lyrics, about yachts, presents from Tiffany's and the like, urging Santa to hurry up with glamorous gifts. It made her chuckle, the more so because it was from her conspicuous consuming sister. "I know, I know," Sandy had written, "it's too much me, isn't it? I know sometimes I have been a real pip, and not exactly Miss Sensitivity when it comes to your situation. But I love you. Please come for Christmas. I won't take no for an answer."

Call it emotional weariness, call it sentimentalism, call it the Holy Spirit, but the invitation opened the floodgates for Carol. People invite us into their lives and we either open the doors of our hearts or shut them out. Families are messy. They are what they are, but worth it, Carol thought. As she listened to the carols, her mind was drawn to the Christmas story and how Jesus' incarnation, his coming to earth, is God's invitation. Life is one big invitation, an invitation to open our hearts to God's presence and experience life in its fullest and most abundant way. Christmas is God's invitation to move beyond jealousies and little hurts and disappointments, to make relationships and not things the center of our lives. This was not the time to refuse an invitation — from her sister or from God. What if Mary had turned God down, hadn't said yes? Isn't that what God is asking of us, to say "yes" to God, and all that flows from that relationship?

Carol picked up the phone. "Sandy, your card was a hoot. Thanks for the invitation. We'll be there." Who knows where this will lead, Carol thought to herself as she hung up. We're still who we are. But somehow, deep in her heart, she knew this Christmas was already special.

Prayer

Gracious God: You came into our world, not where we expected, in royal setting at the heart of the empire, but in an unassuming manger in out of the way Bethlehem. You came among us where we actually live, not where we would like to live. You embraced us as we are, not as we would like to be. So help us to see this night as an invitation, to open our hearts and know what blessings you have for us, this Christmas and always. Amen.

Christmas Calm

"What a moving experience," Mark Sheffield enthusiastically said to his friend Raphael Gonzales as they left the church. He meant it. The two of them occasionally talked religion at work, and when Raphael discovered Mark didn't know about the Latino tradition of *Los Posadas*, he invited him to his church. "Each Advent," Raphael explained, "we re-enact the story of Joseph seeking lodging for his young wife Mary, who is weary from travel and heavy with child. For nine days, young and old take various identities, as the young couple or the innkeeper, processing around the church or through the streets. At each station, an ancient exchange is repeated. You really should come and see." And so he did.

Mark's Spanish wasn't very good, but he grasped the action. Those playing Joseph would approach the inn, knock on the door, and say in a loud voice, "In the name of God, we ask those dwelling here, give to some travelers lodging this evening." And from the inside a chorus of voices responded, "This is not an inn," or "There is no space, move on" or "I cannot open lest you be a scoundrel." As Joseph moved from one inn to the next, the innkeepers grew angry and hostile and the night grew colder. "We are tired," Joseph anxiously implored. Finally he played his trump card, "Please give *posada* — shelter — for this who is the 'queen of heaven' — but still to no avail.

"After building this up for eight nights, the church bristles with anticipation on Christmas Eve," Raphael explained, "That's when Joseph's request finally moves the heart of the innkeeper, who offers the couple all he has left, a stable. Enhanced by the love the innkeeper offers, this humble setting becomes the place of Jesus' birth. Afterward the church breaks out in song and celebration, giving thanks for the generosity of the innkeeper and the *posada* given to Mary and Joseph."

That image of experiencing welcome and finding shelter as central to the Christmas story had never struck Mark so powerfully before. He remembered Raphael saying how difficult it was when his family had first immigrated to the United States when he was ten, and what the welcome, the hospitality of a few meant to him, a stranger in a strange land. The point of the *Los Posadas* tradition was clear, intending to remind the church of how the stranger can be God in disguise — and thus how important it is for us to provide shelter — physical, emotional, spiritual — as did the innkeeper on that first Christmas. But he could not help wonder if his own church would provide shelter even if the holy family itself showed up at their doors on Christmas Eve — Mark knew how the defenses go up when the stranger appears.

Mark discovered something of the importance of finding shelter when his life fell apart six years earlier. He had gone through a messy divorce, made worse by the realization that he had been largely to blame. Yet out of it something positive had happened in his life. He had been a casual churchgoer at best — Christmas, sometimes Easter, and maybe when the kids sang, but he didn't think it had much to do with "real life" as he called it, until his world crumbled and he knew that he needed a firmer foundation. One of his golfing buddies gently lured him back and introduced him to a God so different from that boring, irrelevant, judgmental deity he had created to justify keeping God at arm's length.

Over time Mark plowed into church life with an intensity that surprised even his closest friends. But still, at Christmas, some of his old agitation would return. Watching families prepare, even as he knew his own children, now teenagers, would be in another state for the holidays, plunged him into a loneliness which nearly would sink him. He had once thought that getting religion meant God would fill in all the gaps, eliminating his "issues." But he still struggled with periodic bouts of feeling alienated and alone, uncertain of his place. He had stopped watching the TV Christmas specials, which always touched the emotions, but then discouraged him even more with their depiction of the most complicated family dynamics being resolved into a glorious holiday harmony in an hour. Mark was trying to accept that God doesn't fill all the voids, and sometimes the emptiness remains precisely to keep us longing for something deeper.

But it was hard. Everyone else seemed obsessively busy, rushing around, excited, while he actually had more time come December, a slow time at work. And so he plunged into church activities — the pageant, the Advent workshop, the special cantata.

His office was closed on Christmas Eve, so he decided to see if they needed any help at church. Running into Nancy Stone, the church's energetic new choir director, he inquired innocently enough, "Anything I can do?" "Anything you can do?" she cried, "You better believe it," and before long he was organizing folders, setting up chairs, and bringing music stands. As he watched her scurry around, it dawned on him, now there's a stressful job, requiring the stamina of a prize fighter and the diplomacy of a Henry Kissinger — and to do that job with four children at home. After an already packed Advent, Nancy was stressing over the fact that three of the choir's six sopranos weren't going to be there, effectively eliminating most of the best ideas she had for Christmas music. Mrs. Lundy had offered to sing, "Gesu, Bambino" for a record thirty-second year in a row. She had said everyone was expecting her to sing it, it was a tradition, but Nancy knew what everyone was really expecting was to have the new choir director graciously get Mrs. Lundy, whose voice had seen better days, to bow out. Like choir directors before her Nancy hemmed and hawed but finally decided there were some things more important than musical perfection when it came to Christmas Eve. Mrs. Lundy would get to offer her Christmas gift.

Walking by the church office, Mark overheard Pastor Hendrick's end of an animated phone conversation. "Yes, Lena, I know, I won't forget. I know it's been simmering four hours. Yes, I know you have to use three layers of cheese-cloth. Yes, Lena, I know it's too heavy for you to do it." The next thing he knew Pastor Hendrick was calling after him, "Mark, Mark… can you help me? I've got to get the was-sail ready. Lena just called and gave me my orders." Saint Andrew's church had a long tradition of gathering after the 11 p.m. service for a fellowship time. College students and others in from out of town loved the opportunity to make connections, and the event often went on for an hour or more. Lena was in charge of preparing the Christmas Eve wassail bowl, a mixture of spices and cider prepared accord-ing to her strict instructions. A native of Munich, Lena had emigrated after the war, and tended to run everything with strict Germanic precision. She was the general. And Pastor Hendrick was the chief foot soldier — actually the *only* foot soldier — in her wassail preparations. No one else would do in her mind. So for the next two hours, Mark helped the pas-tor strain fourteen gallons of cider through the cheese cloth. "Gosh, pastor, I didn't know this was in your job descrip-tion." Pastor Hendrick said nothing, but arched his eyebrow, as if to say, you don't know the half of it.

Soon it was time to get to his brother's annual Christmas Eve dinner, an event he half looked forward to, half dreaded. Mark could spot the house from a half mile away. It was always the house with the most Christmas lights. He was welcomed at the door by his niece, wearing a T-shirt with the word "naughty" on it next to a picture of Santa, who was obviously checking his list twice. He spotted his other niece with a similar T-shirt, except hers had the word "nice." The evening was filled with lots of suggestive banter about the sisters "naughty" and "nice." He loved his brother, but being with him made him feel a stranger, an outcast. His brother was cynical about things religious, and in fact was a bit embarrassed by Mark's "awakening." "You're a smart guy. You don't really believe in this stuff, do you? I need to see in order to believe." Mark responded, "You know, bro, you don't believe because you see. Rather you see because you believe." He thought his line rather clever but it fell on deaf ears. "Thanks, but I believe in a secular Christmas. You go to church, but I'm just going to have myself a merry little Christmas right here, with some more eggnog." Mark was more eager than usual to get on to church.

By the time he arrived, the choir was already well into their rehearsal. The hard work the choir put in paid off. "Love Came Down At Christmas" came off beautifully and made his heart soar, and even "Gesu, Bambino" seemed especially touching this year. Pastor Hendrick spoke of the joy of being home for Christmas, and how special this season is when we feel we have a place where we belong. But he reminded the congregation that Jesus was not home for Christmas, his family had difficulty finding shelter, and for Christians the life of faith not only involves finding shelter, or being home for Christmas, it means offering shelter to those who need it most. When they sang "Silent Night," Mark, for the moment, felt all was calm in his world.

As they were hanging up their robes following the service, he could already feel sneaking up on him the anxiety of going to an empty house. His fellow bass, Fred Smoot, perhaps inspired by the message, unexpectedly turned to him and said, "Mark, if you're not going anywhere tomorrow, how about coming to our house for Christmas dinner?" Mark sputtered out a curt refusal, "Thanks, Fred, but it's a family day. You enjoy it." and quickly went to the Fellowship Hall for the wassail bowl. He chatted, visited, and laughed with his fellow church members and then stood for a while at the side, just observing the community in action. Beginning to sink into melancholy, he caught himself, and as he watched the camaraderie, it hit him. This community, these people are my shelter, my *posada*, this is my family, who perhaps understand me better than even those I grew up with. I don't have to keep knocking or keep wondering who would let me in. The community who follows the one who was born a stranger, in a stable, is the community who welcomes and invites and includes.

Spotting Fred across the room, Mark hurried over, "If the invitation is still open, I'd love to join you tomorrow. It is good to be welcomed to your family — and God's."

Prayer

Gracious God: This day help us to hear the good news for all people that is born in Bethlehem, a savior who is Christ the Lord. Help us to be like the innkeeper, ready to offer shelter to those who look for refuge. Help us to be like the angels, offering our unfettered praise. Help us to be like Mary, full of faith and ready to trust. Help us to be like shepherds, willing to go and see what God has done. Help us to be like the wise men, ready to bring our treasures for God's service. Help us to be like the disciples you would have us be. In Jesus' name we pray. Amen.

Christmas Connections

It was Christmas Eve and Adrian Kraft was still at work. Of course, it was his own choosing. Assistant manager at Walmart, he had volunteered to work until the store closed at 11 in order to give others a chance to be with family. Oh, how he wished he could be with family too, but he was experiencing his first Christmas without Joan, his wife of 35 years, who had died in April after a fifteen-month struggle with lymphoma. Adrian knew this was going to be a tough time and decided he'd be better off keeping himself busy. His daughter Sarah and her family were coming in the next week, and his son Randy, who had to work late also would be flying in from Minneapolis on Christmas Day, but for now Adrian was going to be alone.

He had long heard it said that this is the time of the year when solitude is feared the most, and he wanted to guard against the kind of self-pity thinking everyone but he was basking in the glow of holiday merriment. Indeed, in some ways it seemed as though the whole human community labors mightily at Christmas, in all kinds of ways to bring stragglers, like him, under its wing.

Certainly his friends did their best, inviting him to the same Christmas parties he and Joan had always attended. Still he was acutely aware of going solo, uncoupled in a profoundly paired up world.

The store was surprisingly full with folks primarily rushing in to buy those last minute stocking gifts, tubes of toothpaste, gummy bears, and quirky pairs of socks. In Adrian's mind, last minute shoppers were of two kinds — those who are afraid they haven't gotten enough stuff to make the family happy and those who pride themselves on waiting until the end. He watched a family walk up and down the aisles, indecision on their faces. He struck up a conversation. "How about a chia pet? That's a novel gift. What about chia Shrek or chia Garfield?" he suggested none too convincingly. Actually he was thinking to himself "Who in their right mind would want such a thing?" but they still had a lot in stock, and he didn't want to have to send them back to the supplier.

Being in retail created an ongoing dilemma for Adrian. Every year he had to gear himself up to sell more stuff that people really didn't need. After all the economy — and his personal economy — his job — depended on it. But still it made him uncomfortable at times; he couldn't get out of his mind those "WWJD" bracelets they sold a few years back — What would Jesus do? Would Jesus be selling WWJD bracelets? He doubted it. It was part of his job to create want, and he lamented how well his employer did it. He vividly remembered watching a family scurrying behind their five-year-old who was racing from toy to toy, box to box gleeful-ly shouting "I need it, I need it." They innocently asked the boy on the way in what was on his Christmas list and he was telling them. When he wrapped his spindly arms around a box with barbells, they finally came to their senses. "Benji, you don't need that; you don't even know what it is, even though you may think you want it!"

All this effort to make connections with people we love, even find happiness through stuff, weighed heavily on him this year when he was so conscious that the connection he most wanted with Joan was no longer possible. Never be-fore had he been so aware of being alone, disconnected, even when surrounded by crowds of shoppers.

He couldn't help but be nostalgic of Christmas' past. It was a miracle he and Joan got beyond their first Christmas when they had invited his parents for Christmas dinner. Joan was nervous since she wasn't convinced her mother-in-law was very happy about their marriage; moreover, she had never cooked a turkey before. No one told her about taking that stuff out of the innards, and somehow the paper in which the gizzards were wrapped caught fire in the oven and smoke was everywhere. The dinner might still have been rescued if Adrian hadn't gotten the bright idea of grabbing the flaming pan and throwing it out in the backyard, where — guess what? — the dog was ready to have a feast. As he walked inside, proud of his fireman's quickness, both Joan and his mother accosted him, "Adrian, what were you thinking?" — and the women, strangely, bonded out of this incident as his mother told stories of culinary disasters that had befallen her while the two of them cobbled together a quite presentable dinner made up mostly of vegetables.

His reverie was broken by his phone's ringing. It was Randy. "What's up?" "Not much, just getting these last minute shoppers settled. What's up with you?" He could hear the sounds of laughter in the background and figured Randy was at his favorite bar. "Just doing a little Christmas celebrating connecting with my buddies and wanted to wish you a Merry Christmas. I'm looking forward to seeing you — afraid I wasn't that creative in my shopping, but what about if we go out to lunch and a movie while I'm home — my treat?" Adrian simply said "Sounds good," but for him that was a better gift than receiving a new BMW. Their mother's death had been hard on the children too, and though in some ways they grieved alone, the shared loss make their bond even more precious.

Randy's call lifted his spirits and Adrian spent the rest of the evening patrolling the floor, helping customers, serving as the unofficial Walmart "greeter" in spite of himself and his position. He noticed a man who had been there several times before. Adrian's shoppers weren't those who frequented Talbot's or Ralph Lauren. His customers definitely didn't get whatever they got at Jared's. They didn't dine at Ruth Chris'. Adrian had chatted with the man before and knew his family was struggling. He had lost his job at the local GE plant several months ago and with only his wife's salary as a nursing aid, they were worried that they might lose their home. They shopped at Walmart only for necessities and had told their children not to expect much. They were getting only "practical gifts" for Christmas, and indeed, as the man did his last minute shopping, he was buying things like duct tape and T-shirts. Walmart isn't known for fine clothing, but they had gotten a beautiful selection of silk scarves, and several times Adrian noticed the husband came by and eyed a particularly striking blue and red variety and then moved on. "My wife would love this" he said to no one in particular, "but I can't," and Adrian, ever empathetic responded, "It is tough, isn't it?" The man was surprised that Adrian had heard him, but nodded and moved away.

Adrian decided then and there he could do something about that and picked up the scarf, paid for it, and went about his business. As soon as the man got into the checkout line, Adrian took the scarf and whispered to the clerk to sneak it into the man's bags without his seeing. The scheme went off without a hitch. Adrian was pleased with himself and wondered what the man would think when he discovered the package with the simple note on it, "for your wife." It was like being a secret Santa and that connection made him feel less alone.

Finally 11 p.m. came. They closed out quickly and Adrian realized there was still time to catch the final twenty minutes of the candlelight service at his church. He slipped into the last pew, next to Mary Landry, who had been divorced for many years but had recently, to the congregation's surprise and joy, married a teacher in town. The choir was singing "Love Came Down At Christmas," with those simple lyrics:

Love came down at Christmas
Love all lovely, love divine

Love was born at Christmas
Star and angels gave the sign.

Love shall be our token
Love shall be yours and love be mine
Love to God and all men
Love for plea and gift and sign...

After the service, his wife's best friend Helen came up and gave him a big hug and the Francis twins, who had expressed nothing but indifference when he had them in Sunday school, came over to tell him they were now in college and loving it.

When he finally got home, the parade of cars that had come to see the luminaries in his neighborhood were gone, but the candles were still shining. He took a walk and thought about his day, the loneliness and yet the connections he had made. *Love came down at Christmas*, the choir had sung, *connecting heaven and earth.* This season, he pondered, had little to do with gifts, parties, and all the trappings, everything to do with love — the love of God come to earth, the love that connects us with each other. To be sure, the love we give and the love we get is never enough. In many ways we are an empty well needing constant replenishment from the only unfailing source, Jesus, and from his human ambassadors. Love is life's connector, and Adrian saw it clearly: because he had more love to give, he had more life to live. It wasn't a perfect Christmas. It never is. But, still, it was very good.

Prayer

In the stillness of this night, O Lord, love came down to earth and Christ was born. In the stillness of this night, may Christ be born in each one of us again. When we are feeling lost and lonely, may your presence give us comfort. When we are feeling confused and uncertain, may your presence give us direction. When we are wondering what is your purpose for us, may your presence show us we have more love to give. Love came down at Christmas and nothing is ever the same. Praise be to you, O Lord, Emmanuel. Amen.

Necessary Gifts

As always, Bob Smith seemed to be running late. By the time he left the Reinhardt's annual party, it was already 10 p.m., the hour he was supposed to meet the other elders to help prepare communion for the Christmas Eve service. "Look who is finally here, it's Buffalo Bob," he heard Fred Hendrick chuckle as Bob burst through the door. Much to his annoyance, Fred always called him that, an arcane reference only the Baby Boomers in the congregation really understood. The host of the most popular kids TV show of the '50s, the Howdy Doody Show, Buffalo Bob Smith was a silly sort of figure prancing around in his buckskin suit while trying to corral the antics of the likes of Clarabelle the Clown, Flub-a-Dub, and Phineas T. Bluster. Why hadn't his parents given him a dignified name, like Harrison J. Smith? When Fred learned Buffalo Bob Smith was a Presbyterian too — well, that just solidified his little joke about Pineville Presbyterian Church's veteran elder.

Bob wasn't a sour person — in fact people generally thought him a positive spirit — but it seemed as though little things were irritating him more, especially at Christmas. At church it always seemed to him that they were expecting him to pick up the pieces — and if he were a few minutes late, just get over it. Listening to Garrison Keillor describe Christmastime in Lake Wobegon as a series of small disasters, Bob was beginning to agree.

Earlier that day Bob had gotten into a squabble with Becky, his wife of 34 years. She was preparing a turkey with cornbread stuffing, a pan of sweet potatoes, and a bowl of cranberry relish to take to Ted and Joanne's house, her brother and sister-in-law. "You know how hard it is for us to travel with Ted's emphysema," Joanne had told her. "And our kids with their young babies, it's just easier if you come here for Christmas dinner." That sounded good, except Joanne was rather skilled at parceling out most of the responsibilities to other family members. "Becky, you wouldn't mind doing the turkey, would you? You know I don't eat meat" — and it wasn't only food. On Tuesday she called and asked if she could use Becky's good china, and by Thursday it was, "Why don't you bring the red goblets too? They go so well with the china." Not only did Becky find herself preparing most of the meal; it was double the work hauling it by car. Joanne wound up contributing the likes of a kale and cucumber soufflé — healthy to be sure, but almost inedible.

Becky was grumbling, "This isn't fair," and Bob finally said, "Well then, why don't we just stay home with the kids like we say we're going to do every year?" "No, we can't do that. Christmas is family time," Becky insisted. "We need to be together." "Dysfunctional though we are," Bob muttered, seeing her scowl at him, as he walked away.

He felt a little guilty at his irritation. He did love Becky and her determination to make family work, even when it was hard. He left the house to look for her Christmas gift; he was late at that too. He had tried earlier but couldn't find the right thing and just wasn't good at this. Becky was so much better than he. And though she always expressed gratitude at his gift, Bob did notice that more often than not the gifts he got ended up in the exchange line on December 26. "Oh, I love it, but if I can just get a slightly darker color it would be perfect," she would say.

The communion preparers were nearly finished cutting the bread, so Bob took off his coat and poured the juice into the chalice, wondering as he did why they had to have communion on Christmas Eve anyway — the Baptists and Methodists didn't, and having communion meant he not only had to come early, but then had to stay late to clean up. And since Christmas Eve was a Saturday, the minister would probably expect him to be in church again on Sunday morning — a bit much, don't you think? But he caught himself, irritated that he was so irritable on what was supposed to be a holy, sacred night. He carried the elements into the sanctuary where he noticed how beautiful the decorations were. Effie Leffingwell had outdone herself this time, he thought, as he gazed at the incredible tree of poinsettias, topped by a cross surrounded by a wreath. Chet, the longtime custodian, was painstakingly lighting the ranks of candelabra. The sanctuary sparkled.

It was time to settle into the service, to contemplate once again on this night the mystery of the incarnation. Becky always told him he thought too much and overanalyzed everything making it more complicated than it needed to be. Her religion was more practical — be kind, do unto others as you would have them do to you, love your neighbor. But Bob couldn't help it. It was just who he was, trying to figure things out like how could it be that God became human?

Their young pastor, Ray Francis — Bob couldn't get used to the fact that he was about the age of his son — began to explain that communion itself helped illustrate the incarnation. Both offered the promise of God with us, and the understanding of both depended on our receptivity. Both necessitate that we become as little children, full of wonder and expectation. Communion requires us to be fed like children and to literally come to the table with our arms outstretched and our hands open, empty. We come ready to receive that which feeds us. Without that spirit, Ray contended, Jesus' incarnation is simply dead history. We can sing, "O come, O come Emmanuel," but the truth of God with us only happens when we come with open hand and open heart.

After the sermon, Bob took his place at the communion table holding the bread while Pastor Ray held the cup. As the communicants came down the aisle, Bob felt his heart softening as he considered the ties that bound him to nearly every person — there was Jack Sprague who had given his parents fits as a teenager, helping his ailing mother down the aisle; there was Betty Fulkerson, still grieving the loss this past year of her beloved Peter, barely able to hold her tears back as she opened her hands to receive; there came Millie and Milton Nash, 57 years married, with a host of grandchildren trailing behind them. "The body of Christ... given for you... the blood of Christ shed for you" each one heard.

From the corner of his eye Bob saw Lenny start down the aisle, unsteady, unkempt, struggling. Lenny was part of a group of homeless men whom the community churches had been housing during the winter months. Some of them had begun coming to church, which frankly didn't make everyone happy; they often smelled of stale alcohol and dirty clothes, and they looked a little wild. "We've given them shelter... isn't that enough?" some were heard to whisper. "Do they have to come to church?"

As Lenny made his way down the aisle, unshaven, disheveled, obviously having fallen off the wagon again, he was muttering something. Bob couldn't make out the words at first, but as he got closer Lenny's cry became distinct, "I'm not worthy, I've blown it again, I shouldn't be here, I'm not worthy." Bob found his gaze riveted on Lenny's face as he protested his very presence there. But he kept coming. As he stretched out his trembling hand toward the bread, he was still lamenting, "I'm not worthy, I'm not worthy." Pastor Ray learned down to whisper in his ear, "None of us is worthy, Lenny, but we have a God of grace, who loves us, and forgives us when we fall. God lifts us up and gives us chance after chance. So come, Lenny, with open hands and receive and join the community of the unworthy who are ever lifted up by the worthiness of Christ alone."

"Merry Christmas," Bob shouted to Fred and the others as he left after cleaning up following the service. At that moment, it seemed clear. The miracle of Christmas, of the incarnate Christ, of God with us, was the miracle of grace — God reaching out and offering his love, and all we have to do is come with open hands and open hearts. Somehow, Bob knew as he drove home that even the dinner at Joanne and Ted's house on Christmas Day was going to be just fine.

Prayer

Gracious and compassionate God: Amid the poinsettias and candles and sweet smell of the greens, help us to find our way to the manger once again, and meet anew the Christ Child. In Jesus, you welcome us, not because we are worthy, but because of your love. In Jesus, you reach out to us, not because we deserve it, but because you have compassion for us. In Jesus, you touch us with your presence, not because we are perfect disciples but because you care for the lost and lonely of the world. Help us this Christmas to find joy in the midst of all of life's messiness, to find hope in the midst of a world which too easily gets discouraged. This we pray in Jesus' name. Amen.

Lost and Found

It had been a tough time for the Marston family. They had lost their fourteen-year-old Irish Setter just after Thanksgiving and they were all still grieving. Madison had been the glue and although she had become increasingly frail, she hadn't lost that feisty, rambunctious, lovable spirit. It had been particularly tough on eleven-year-old Max, the most ardent animal lover of the family. Madison had awakened him every morning by jumping on his bed and bathing him with big slobbery kisses. That lathering of his son's face made his father Doug uneasy. "Who knows what she's gotten into before she licks you?" he'd mutter. He liked a well-behaved animal who sat at your feet and came when called. Max's mother Rachel and teenage sister Cynthia welcomed Madison's affection and unconditional love, but they too were concerned with germs.

Not Max. He loved animals of all kinds and counted gerbils, turtles, frogs, fish, hamsters, and white mice among his pets. A suburban kid, he loved going to his aunt's farm and spending hours in the barn. It was not surprising that his favorite part of the Christmas story was the birth in the manger. He somehow couldn't see that humble setting as much of a sacrifice — sheep, goats, camels, donkeys — what could be better than all those barnyard smells, rubbing up against their warm fur, seeing their breath expelled into the frosty night air?

"Why don't they ever show dogs at the manger?" he asked his Sunday school teacher, and when she said there was simply no evidence for that, he argued to the contrary. "What shepherd doesn't have a good sheepherding dog to help him in his job? You think they would have left their dogs back in the field?" When he told his mother about this encounter, she had to agree. And then, worthy of a college art major, she pulled out an old textbook and showed him several Renaissance era paintings that did indeed show dogs at the manger.

So although Madison's death hit Max hardest, when Rachel suggested they go to the mall for some Christmas shopping, all jumped at the chance for something to lift their spirits. Cynthia and her mother took off for Nordstrom's and the Gap, Max and his dad headed for Dick's Sporting Goods and Radio Shack. They agreed to meet at the food court in an hour for hot chocolate and a Famous Amos™ cookie.

They weren't prepared for what happened next. As they slurped up the whipped cream on their hot chocolate, suddenly a college age woman seated next to them popped up and started singing "Joyful, Joyful, We Adore You," followed by an older man off to their left, then others in groups of two or three. As soon as that was over, four men riding the escalator began to sing "O Come All Ye Faithful." Shoppers congregated to see what was happening, and some, when they knew the words, joined in. "Is this one of those 'flash mobs' we read about?" Doug said to Rachel. "Could be," she said, before joining in the chorus herself. From the third floor of the mall, a powerful tenor voice belonging to a very tall man hanging over the rail, began "Go Tell It On The Mountain," and soon hundreds were singing. There was quiet for just a brief moment before strains of "O Holy Night" began. Slowly a young couple dressed as Mary and Joseph came to the center of the food court and even tattooed highly pierced teenagers hanging out at the mall found their way over to look reverently at the baby. It was all over in ten minutes, and then, robot-like, the fiercely focused shoppers drifted back into the stores. But, at least for a moment, those who may have lost their way in the rush for goods, had found their way to an impromptu community of faith prompted by the birth of Jesus.

"That was fun," the family agreed as they began the twenty-minute ride back home. As they pulled into their driveway, a small dog scooted in front of them, and Doug had to swerve to avoid him. "Watch it, Dad," Cynthia shouted. "I am," Doug responded somewhat impatiently. They brought their purchases in and then settled in front of the TV to watch "Modern Family," which as Doug carefully reminded them each week, wasn't much like their family — thankfully.

During a quiet moment they heard whimpering outside, and when they went to investigate, there was a tired, cold, 57 variety Benji-like dog shivering under the holly bush, eyes bright, but forlorn. It was the dog they had almost clipped. "He's lost," Max said firmly, and "we can't let him stay out there in the cold like that." Before long he was in the family room, wrapped in towels, having had a bath and been fed, enjoying Max's attentive brushing.

"He can stay in the laundry room tonight," Doug declared, though Max tried to make his case for letting him sleep in his room, "and tomorrow we'll see if we can find his owner."

The next day was Saturday, and Doug right away called the SPCA and the town offices to see if anyone had reported a missing dog. Nothing! "Can't we keep him?" Max asked, already knowing the answer. "Just think about how his owners feel about losing their dog. How would you feel?" Max knew his father was right, but when they went to put "Lost dog" signs up a mile in all directions, he was tempted to follow after and pull them back down, hoping against hope no one would call.

When they got home Max asked to no one in particular, "What do you think we should name him?" "We're not naming him anything. We're not going to get attached. He's not our dog," his father said decisively.

This stray quickly won their hearts, overcoming an initial shyness, and eagerly nuzzling up to the latest person to enter the room. Max got out the old leash and volunteered to walk him when he got home from school. After a couple of days, his dad relented, and let their canine guest stay in the kitchen, and in a few more days — no surprise — he found a place in Max's room.

No one wanted to slip into this comfortable acceptance. Rachel had been resistant to getting a new dog. Her parents, two hours away, were having health problems and she anticipated more weekend family visits there. It wasn't the time to think of getting attached. But somehow it just happened.

Then they got the call Max dreaded, just three days before Christmas. "Do you have a short grey and white haired terrier type dog? A friend saw your sign and we think you may have found Mertz," the excited voice on the line said. The Marstons were less than excited as they bundled up and prepared to return their stray. But there was plenty of joy in Joe and Heather Denton's home when they reunited with Mertz, whom they had named after Fred Mertz, the curmudgeonly neighbor in the old "I Love Lucy" show, though both families agreed that didn't fit his temperament at all. He was such a sweet dog. The families chatted a while and the Dentons thanked them profusely for finding Mertz and taking such good care of him.

"It's good we helped that couple find their lost dog, don't you think?" Doug offered as they drove home, and they all agreed, if a little grudgingly. Their low mood hadn't lifted as they went to the Christmas Eve service a couple of days later. They were a little surprised to find themselves singing "Amazing Grace" as one of the "carols," but understood when their pastor started talking about Christmas as a time of being "lost" and "found." "God is always searching for us, reaching out to us, inviting us," he said. "God is the hound of heaven, who keeps after us until we find that place where we are intended to be, in God's family, loved and cared for. God came to us at Christmas as a vulnerable, defenseless baby, like one of us, and lived like us, and experienced pain and suffering like us — so we could understand God is not removed from us, but is with us, 'Emmanuel.' We live in a world which sometimes seems lost, but even in those moments when we experience the most inexplicable darkness, even in those moments God desires us to find our way home to his compassionate embrace, an embrace that often takes place through the hands of others reaching out to help. In some sense we are all lost, trying to find a way home in the darkness, but the joy of Christmas is the knowledge that we are found. We have a home in the light."

Max broke the ice on the way home, "Was anyone else thinking about Mertz during the sermon?" "Uh-uh," they all muttered in unison. "I'm glad we helped find his owners. It feels good to help someone find their way home." And then after a few minutes of silence, "Was the pastor telling us that we all need a little help in finding our way home — back to God?" Rachel glanced knowingly at Doug, gratified that their son, often seemingly oblivious to anything spiritual, sometimes really got it.

Christmas morning it surprised no one when, after they had opened their gifts, Rachel said, "I think we should make a trip to the SPCA on Saturday. There are a lot of lost dogs there waiting to be found, who need a home filled with love." They all practically jumped with joy. The parable of the lost and found was complete.

Prayer

Lord Jesus, because we could not come to you, you came to us. Because we were lost, you found us. Because we could not find our way home, you showed us the way. This night our joy is full, our hope is fulfilled, our yearning is met with your great grace, for the word has become flesh and dwelt among us, full of grace and truth. Alleluias fill our hearts and we are grateful. Amen.

Baby Blessings

It was an eight hour drive from St. Louis to her parents' home in Akron, Ohio, but MacKenzie McPherson was in no rush. She was both eager to see them and yet dreading it at the same time. It had taken some doing but she had managed to get three days off before Christmas, despite the fact that she worked at Target. She was glad to get out of there, not only because the customers got crazier the closer you got to Christmas, but because the company's credit card breech, which some feared had happened internally, had made everyone edgy.

Although she hadn't seen her family in eight months, and normally would be singing her way home with anticipation, this time was different. She was five months pregnant and hadn't yet said a thing to them, though they talked on the phone regularly. After all she wasn't married, and they weren't going to be very happy about this news.

MacKenzie came from good Scotch Irish stock, long on duty and discipline, not much on emotional warmth. Her mother, Margie, was a worrier who kept everything inside. She worried about whether she was getting the right gifts. Would her four-year-old grandson like the Legos or prefer something electronic? Would the guests she was having over for Christmas Eve dinner be disappointed in her oyster stew? Did she wear the right clothes to the garden club holiday social? Would her husband Mark hold on to his job during economic downturn? You name it. She would worry. Now MacKenzie had given her mother something to really worry about.

Actually if truth be known, her mother and father had long been anxious about her. She was the middle child, the cut up, the one who never wanted to play by the rules. Marty, older by three years, filled her role as the eldest child perfectly — hard worker, good student, walking the straight and narrow, now happily married with two full-of-life children. Always doing it the right way. Her eighteen-year-old younger brother Mike (all the family had names beginning with M — The McPherson clan, her father would announce, putting on a Scottish brogue — Mark, Margie, Marty, MacKenzie, and Mike — she was only glad her parents hadn't named her "Muffy" — or some frilly name Baby Boom parents were wont to do, in the eyes of his sisters), was spoiled rotten, of course, as older siblings always think. Yet in fact Mike was a laid back, conscientious student who had found a focus in sports, especially basketball.

But MacKenzie, though not a bad kid, got into more trouble than her brother and sister combined and just couldn't seem to concentrate when it came to schoolwork. She tried college for a while, compiling a distinctly mediocre record, and dropped out after three semesters when her father told her he was not going to support her "party life" any longer.

She went to work but seemed to change jobs as often as boyfriends. "You're a narcissist" one of the boys told her when they broke up. She wasn't sure what it meant, but knew it wasn't flattering. It was no wonder that her parents worried about her being able to settle into stability. When she decided to follow her boyfriend of three months to St. Louis where he was starting a new job, they weren't happy. "What can we do?" Mark muttered to himself, "It's her life. She's an adult." And to Margie, "You've got to let her go, stop worrying." But of course, she didn't.

That relationship fell apart but MacKenzie stayed, making a few friends, hanging onto a mundane job that barely made ends meet, securing a thirteen-year-old car that was forever on the verge of breaking down.

And now this, pregnant at 24, certainly not by design. She was always so careful. She hardly knew this guy, but after a few too many adult beverages, well, things just happened. She kept hoping the home pregnancy test was wrong, but when friends suggested an abortion, she couldn't do it. It's no big deal, they told her, but MacKenzie knew too many people for whom it was.

A baby really changes everything, she knew. She had heard her mother say that many times. How in the world could she survive this? The relationship had been too casual to expect much support there. She'd be dealing with the baby largely on her own. Frankly, it scared her. She never even really liked babysitting. Some girls just gravitated toward it, but not she. Babies were too messy, too disruptive.

To amuse herself during the long drive, she put in the *Duck Dynasty* Christmas CD she had gotten. She started laughing as the Robertsons' sang "Duck the Halls" and "Camouflage and Christmas Lights." She found the show campy enough to strike her fancy and was amazed to see the explosion of Duck stuff which flooded the holiday sales market. Indeed, for Christmas she had bought Mike *Duck Dynasty* Boxer shorts, the perfect gift, she thought, until patriarch Phil's remarks about religion stirred up controversy and made her realize gift buying was sometimes fraught with danger. She certainly didn't want to be associated with anything narrow minded, and frankly didn't want a heavy dose of judgment flooding in on her either.

She wasn't proud of her situation. It was an embarrassment, but she still yearned for compassion, not condemnation. MacKenzie had grown up in the church, and though largely disconnected, she knew the stories. She got to thinking about that unwed biblical mother, expecting a baby. How would she have handled the whispers and ridicule? "A child of the Holy Spirit? Who did she think she was kidding?"

At least Mary had the support of Joseph, who though himself was surely subject to gossip, had stuck with Mary and followed what God told him to do.

It was after dinner when MacKenzie arrived home. There was no hiding that she was pregnant. The baby bump was obvious. She steeled herself for the encounter, prepared to be tough, but as soon as she walked in she dissolved in tears. Though she always tried to act strong, adult, in control, especially around her parents, she knew how vulnerable she was, how alone she felt.

Maybe it was the tears or maybe it was just how tiny, how wounded she seemed to them at that moment, but Margie and Mark just embraced her, cried with her, let down their Scottish reserve. No John the Baptist denunciations. No "Didn't we tell you this would happen?" No "How could you do this to us?" "We'll get through this," they said simply and then Margie reminded her of a lesson she had learned from Fred Rodgers of the TV "Neighborhood" fame. "He said, whenever he dealt with things that scared him, or seemed to overwhelm him, his mother would tell him, 'Look for the helpers. In any frightening situation, there are always helpers.' We know there will be helpers for you, us, and others too."

MacKenzie was still a bit anxious as she went off to the Christmas Eve services a couple of days later. She wondered whom her parents had told, and how they would receive her. She was relieved when she felt nothing but warmth from the Ralstons, Fredericks, Perullos, and even from her old Sunday school teacher, Mr. Rainsfords, to whom she had given fits. She suspected they knew when Mrs. Fredericks said, "I imagine this is a special Christmas for you, MacKenzie. We want you to know we love you"

Nestled in between Margie and Mark, MacKenzie felt secure and safe, at least for now. Her world had been rocked, but as she listened to the Christmas story and sang the Christmas carols, she thought that perhaps the baby of Bethlehem could be her own rock. As the soloist sang "A Baby Changes Everything" it seemed as though she was singing right to her. A baby changes everything, my baby — God's baby. Her life was messy, but so was Jesus' birth — this unmarried young woman, who had known not a man, to use the biblical euphemism, whose fiancé was ready to put her away, until startled by his own angel visitation, having to travel to Bethlehem, where they found no room and had to give birth in a stable, being forced to flee to Egypt. This was messy stuff for the one who was the Savior of the world. The birth of a baby is messy, life is messy, but what enables us to survive and thrive is the assurance of Emmanuel — that God is with us. MacKenzie, at least for the moment, felt secure in God's love and knew she was not alone. With the caring people — and Jesus — she could get through this. And the baby would be a blessing.

Prayer

On this magical night when we hear again the good news of the coming of a Savior who is Christ the Lord, we are grateful that you came to us in the form of a baby, fragile, vulnerable, and needy. You continue to come to us when we are lost, confused, or feeling alone. You come to us in the midst of all our messiness to bring hope and strength, to assure us, often through those caring people in our lives, of your love and compassion. This night our joy is full, our hope is fulfilled, our yearning is met with your great grace, for the word has become flesh and dwelt among us, full of grace and truth. Alleluias fill our hearts and we are grateful. Amen.

www.ingramcontent.com/pod-product-compliance
Lightning Source LLC
Chambersburg PA
CBHW071841020426
42331CB00007B/1808